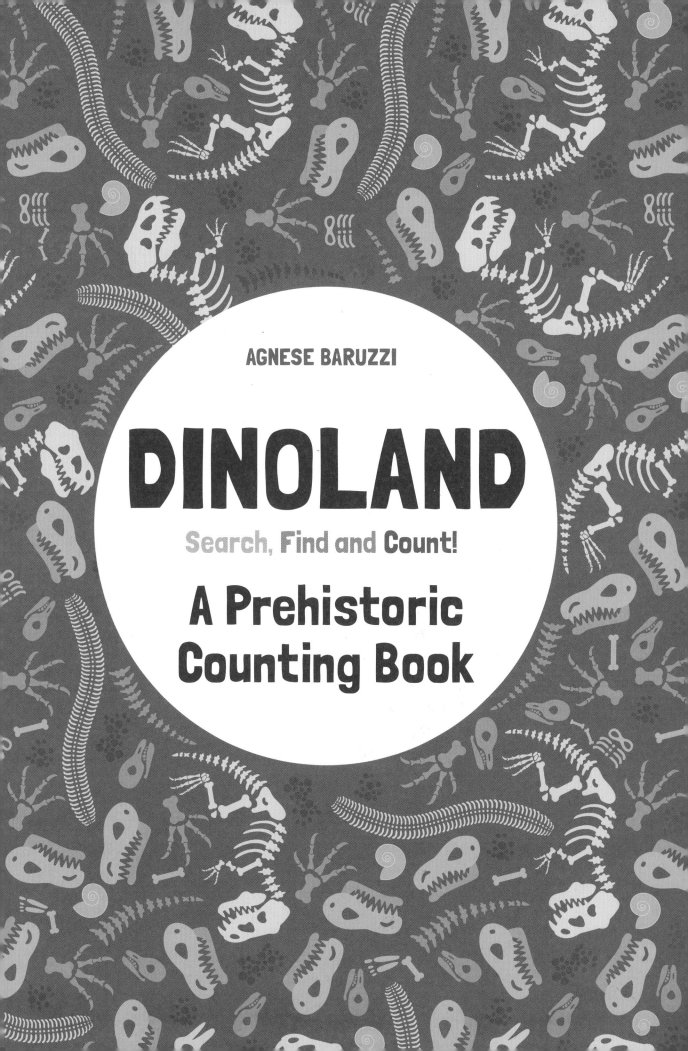

AGNESE BARUZZI

DINOLAND

Search, Find and Count!

A Prehistoric Counting Book

INTRODUCTION

Welcome, young paleontologist. I hope your journey through time was pleasant! It is not every day that we are transported backwards in time to about 230 million years ago!

ARE YOU READY TO DIVE INTO THE PAGES OF THIS BOOK TO EXPLORE THE MYSTERIOUS AND DANGEROUS MESOZOIC AGE?

Well, it is important to remind you that cold blood and courage will not be your only weapons: you will have to resort to your intelligence and your ability to observe! In these pages you will be called on to find and count dozens of dinosaurs, large and small, placid and ferocious, herbivorous and carnivorous.

HOW MANY CREATURES AWAIT YOU, actually, NO ONE KNOWS... as an ASPIRING PALEONTOLOGIST it is YOUR task to track them down and count them all! HERE'S HOW YOU'RE GOING TO DO IT...

Next to each challenge you will find a list of dinosaurs and other prehistoric creatures, followed by a white box.

YOUR TASK WILL BE TO FIND EACH CREATURE AND COUNT THE TOTAL, AND THEN WRITE THE NUMBER IN THE BOX.

Finally, add all your answers: when you go to the last pages, you will be able to compare the numbers you got with the numbers given in the solutions.
IF THEY MATCH, IT'S DONE! All tracked dinosaurs can be properly catalogued, but if the result is wrong, be ready: THE HUNT WILL HAVE TO START AGAIN!

BUT YOUR MISSION DOES NOT END HERE.
There's a family that needs your help!
MOM AND DAD DINO HAVE LOST THEIR EGGS AND THEY ARE TERRIBLY WORRIED.

On each page, hidden amidst dozens of dinosaurs, you will find one of the eggs.
Please try to retrieve all 17 of them and, if you miss even one, look for it in the final pages of the book.
Are you ready for the **BABY DINOSAUR RESCUE MISSION?**

TURN THE PAGE AND START PLAYING!

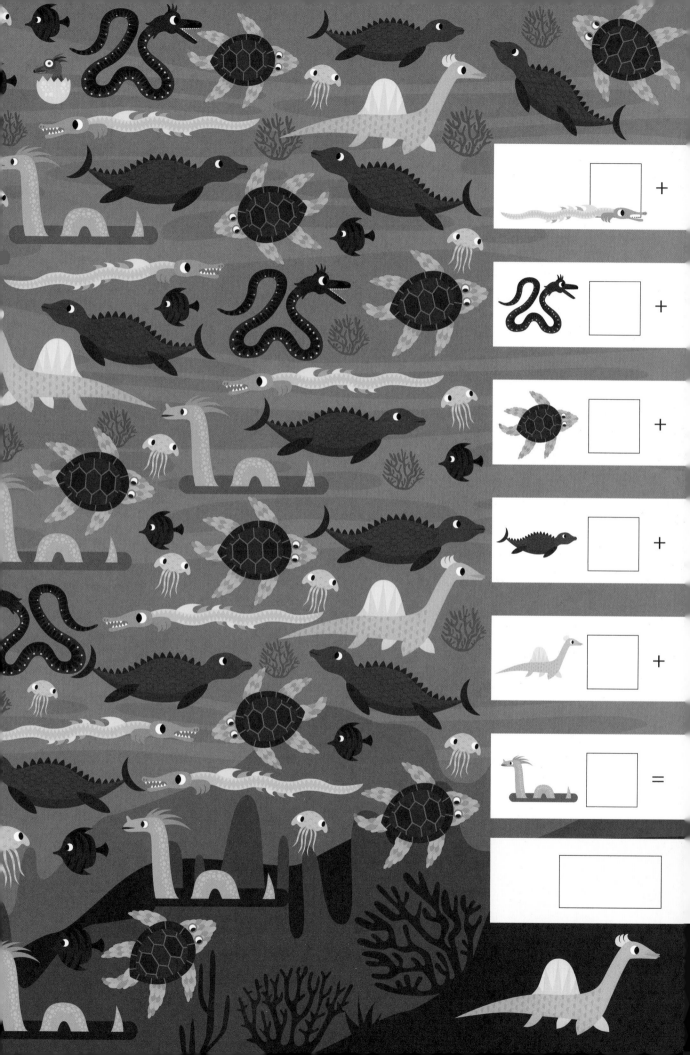

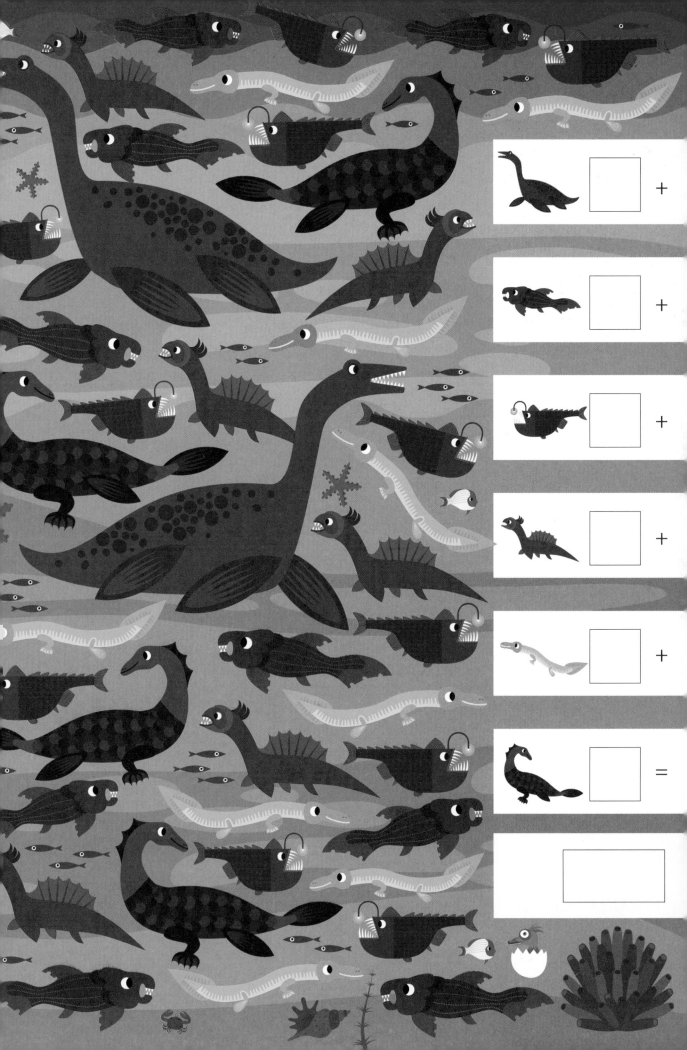

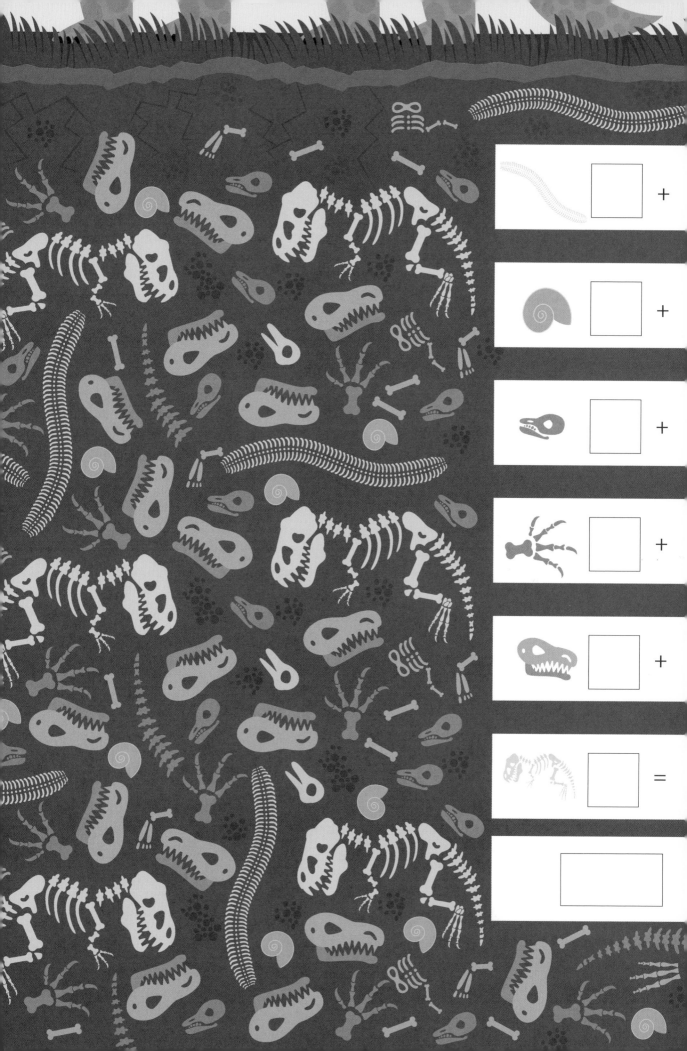

Have you found
ALL OF US?

CHECK IT OUT HERE

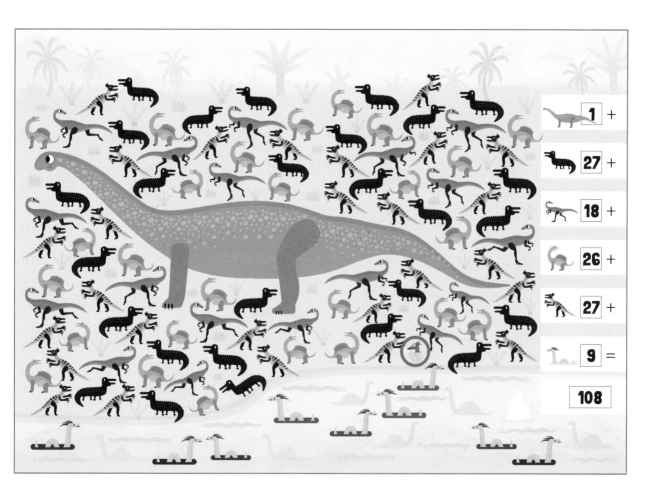

4 +
6 +
3 +
6 +
9 +
9 =

37

14 +
26 +
18 +
14 +
28 +
13 =

113

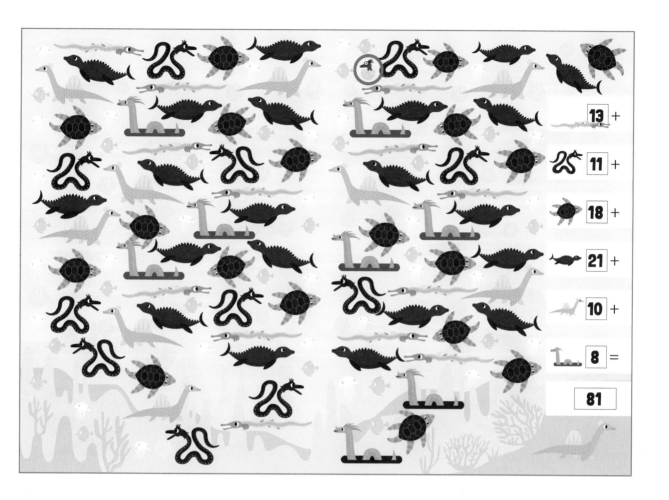

13 +
11 +
18 +
21 +
10 +
8 =

81

21 +
17 +
22 +
17 +
14 +
16 =

107

19 +
13 +
20 +
14 +
14 +
15 =
95

11 +
10 +
14 +
9 +
11 +
10 =
65

13 +
15 +
24 +
22 +
20 +
12 =

106

16 +
18 +
16 +
7 +
18 +
20 =

95

18 +
31 +
34 +
20 +
17 +
26 =
146

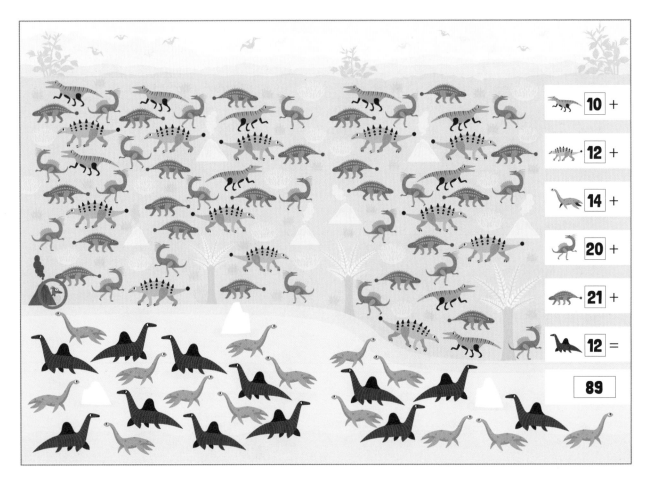

10 +
12 +
14 +
20 +
21 +
12 =
89

4 +
18 +
29 +
15 +
22 +
9 =

97

13 +
16 +
16 +
21 +
11 +
17 =

94

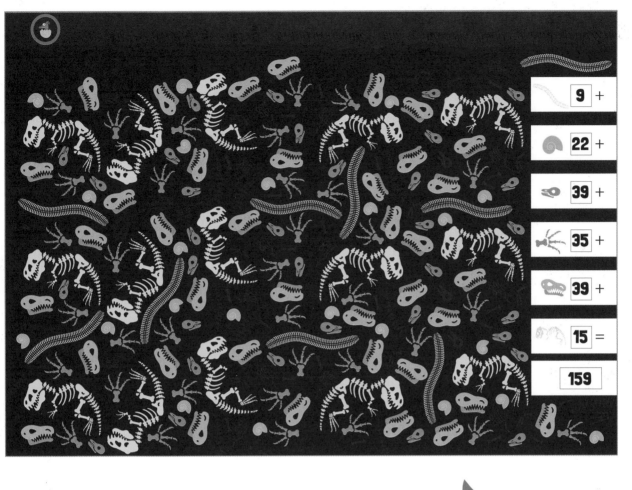

9 +
22 +
39 +
35 +
39 +
15 =

159

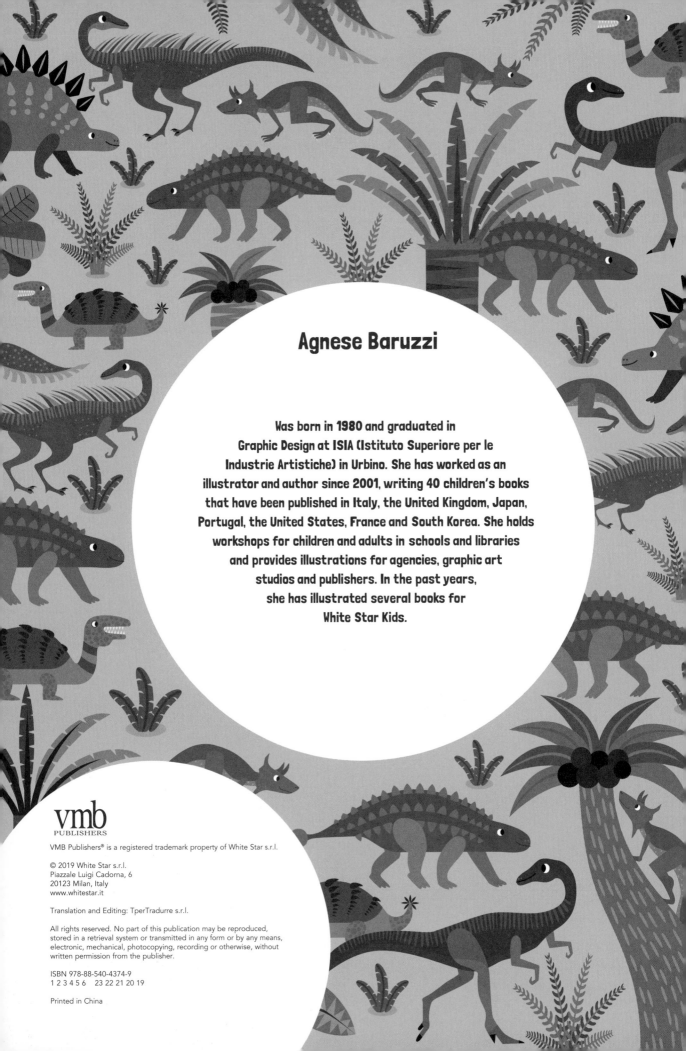

Agnese Baruzzi

Was born in **1980** and graduated in
Graphic Design at **ISIA** (Istituto Superiore per le
Industrie Artistiche) in Urbino. She has worked as an
illustrator and author since **2001**, writing 40 children's books
that have been published in Italy, the United Kingdom, Japan,
Portugal, the United States, France and South Korea. She holds
workshops for children and adults in schools and libraries
and provides illustrations for agencies, graphic art
studios and publishers. In the past years,
she has illustrated several books for
White Star Kids.

vmb
PUBLISHERS

VMB Publishers® is a registered trademark property of White Star s.r.l.

© 2019 White Star s.r.l.
Piazzale Luigi Cadorna, 6
20123 Milan, Italy
www.whitestar.it

Translation and Editing: TperTradurre s.r.l.

ISBN 978-88-540-4374-9
1 2 3 4 5 6   23 22 21 20 19

Printed in China